This book was first published in South-Africa in 2010 by Daniel Berg.

Copyright © 2010 Daniel Berg

All copyright is reserved by the author. No duplication of this material or pictures in this book may be performed without the prior written permission of the author.

ISBN 9780620434997

Illustrator: Sonette Ferreira
Graphic Designer: Jenny Maccallum

This book has been written to serve as a means for parents to relay certain life principles to their children in a simple and understandable way.

In the increasingly fast paced world that we live in, it is now more important than ever before that parents demonstrate their love to their children by saying it to them and by talking to them about the important things in life. I hope that this book will assist you in helping to explain some of life's core principles. Soli Deo Gloria!

For

Diaan and Ané

Tick-tick-tick...
(A story of Persistence)

Once upon a time, a long, long time ago, there was a beautiful valley with green grass, blue streams and huge trees...

In this valley all kinds of animals lived together. There were also many birds. They lived in the branches of the huge old trees.

To the one side of the valley there was a waterfall, and beside the waterfall grew an enormous oak tree.

And, high up in the branches of this old oak tree, a wonderful thing was happening...

The only thing one could hear, was 'tick – tick – tick'. Now what could it be? It was most definitely not the shhhhhhhhsound of the waterfall, nor was it the whoooooooo-sound of the wind howling.

It was a totally new sound.
The sound was coming from the direction of the Owl's nest. Yes, that's right, this tick-tick sound was the sound of a little baby owl pecking at his eggshell.

For hours the little owl pecked away. Tick-tick-tick... Without stopping, he kept on pecking. Mama Owl didn't try to help him to crack the shell, for she knew it was VERY important for the little owl to do it all by himself as it will make him strong and teach him to work hard.

After e few hours of tick-tick-ticking... suddenly... Crrrrrr ..a crack appeared in the shell! And, one, two three, in a jiffy, a small hole could be seen in the shell.

OOoooooohhh, Mama Owl was so excited! The next moment she saw a tiny little beak sticking through the hole in the shell. The little beak kept on working at the shell and soon, before very long, the entire shell had been broken open and there stood a tiny little owl birdie looking at the world outside with a huge grin!

Oooooo, Mama Owl was SO pleased to see him! Oh, all right, he was not one of the prettiest birds, for he did not have feathers, but his mommy loved him just as he was. She knew he would soon grow beautiful feathers. She was especially proud of him because he kept on pecking at his shell for such a long time... until he managed to make a tiny hole in the shell. He never gave up even though he felt very, very tired.

Mama Owl then covered the little owl with her large, soft wing, pulled him tightly against her warm body and decided to call him "Ollie".

Ollie learns to fly
(A story of Ownership)

Since very small, Ollie happened to be a very curious little owl. He always wanted to try out new things. Every day he greedily gulped all the tiny worms which his mom brought him. Sometimes Mommy brought a small grasshopper or some bugs to the nest and then Ollie quickly gobbled them up as fast as he could. But, oh dear, because he did not always remember to chew his food first, he sometimes nearly choked!

When this happened, Mommy Owl had to hold his wings up in the air and beat him lightly on his back until he got his breath back. Mommy Owl then told him in a strict voice, "Ollie, you have to chew your food before you swallow!"

Each day Ollie grew a little bigger. Everyday his feathers grew a little more and his wings also grew larger. His tiny voice also grew louder day by day and the little squeaking noises gradually turned to Twiiiiiiiiieeeeeeettttt sounds.

One morning, Papa Owl said to Ollie, "Ollie, the time has come for you to learn how to fly."

"Yippieeeeeeee!" Ollie shouted, thinking to himself: Oh my, that's going to be a lot of fun!

"What do I have to do, Dad?" Ollie wanted to know.

"Come with me," Dad replied and together the two of them walked to the furthest point of the branch on which their nest was.

When they reached the far end, Ollie looked down and got a huge fright. It was a very long way to the ground! All of a sudden he became very afraid.

"Ollie," his Dad said, "I want you to jump off this branch, to the ground."

"Wh-h-h-a-a-a-t?" Ollie squealed in a small voice. "No, now wait a minute, Dad. You see, Dad, I think there is a much easier way to learn to fly."

"Oh, really?" Dad smiled. "And what might that be?"

"Er...er... see, Dad, I thought we could first climb down to the ground and then I will start running very fast...and then... I'll start moving my wings up and down very quickly... and after a while I will start rising up into the air! I KNOW it will work, Dad, because I have seen that's how the geese do it!"

"No, my lad. You must remember one thing: YOU are NOT a goose. You are an Owl and owls don't fly that way. An Owl must be able to dive down onto its prey at lightning speed; he doesn't have time to run before he starts flying."

"Bbbuut Dad, this looks so high from here, o-o-o-, my tummy feels queasy if I just look down..."

"I'll tell you what, my boy." Close your eyes. Just remember one thing: You must believe you CAN do it, and know that your dad will not let you fall."

Ollie shut his eyes tightly, flapped his wings wildly and

J
U
M
P
E
D

right off the branch.

"**A**-a-a--h-h-h-h-h, a-a-a-a-h-h-h-h!" he yelled, falling like a stone.

But before he had even fallen halfway, his Daddy dived

D
    O
        W
            N

Caught him in the air, and brought him back to the branch.

"Did you see? You didn't get hurt." Ollie dad said.

"But, Dad, I never even flew!"

""That's true, you did not, but you tried and that's the most important thing. The more you try, the better you will do."

Again Ollie jumped, and once again Dad had to rescue him.

"Aw gee, " Ollie sighed when he reached the branch once more. "It didn't work this time either!"

"Ollie, do you want to know something? When I was as small as you are now, I wasn't able to fly either."

"Really, Dad? But how did you manage to become so good?"

"Well, I knew that the ONLY one that could help me, would be ME. NOBODY ELSE can do that for me. So I kept on trying and trying until one day, I got it right!"

"In other words, no one else will do it for me?"

"No."

"So I will have to fly all by myself if I want to fly, Dad?"

"You've got it."

Ollie kept silent for a long while, then he said,

"Well, okay then. If you will help me, Dad, I'll try and try until I get it right."

After many tries that day, something wonderful happened: Ollie
stopped falling! He started gliding... and after another few days of practising, he managed to fly short distances!

Not long after that, Ollie was able to fly very well and he even started doing some tricks in the air! **Wow!**

Ollie learned: if an owl wants to something very much, he must be willing to work very hard and make a lot of mistakes while he learns.

Ollie learns to hunt
(A story of Delayed Gratification)

One day, Papa Owl decided the time has come for Ollie to learn to hunt. As you all know, owls love eating mice and other small animals.

"Come on, Ollie! Today I'm going to teach you how to hunt," Papa Owl said.

"Yippiiieeeeeee!" Ollie shouted, "I can't wait, Dad!"

Ollie and his dad flew through the valley, over the stream, higher and higher, over the treetops... until they reached the mountain.

There they sat on a branch of a very high tree.
At first the Papa Owl just sat there, silent and calm, looking all around him.

"All rightee, Dad! I'm ready for action! What do we do now?" Ollie asked excitedly.

"Now we wait," Papa Owl replied undisturbed.

"But what are we waiting for?" Ollie wanted to know

"You'll see, Ollie. Just be calm and wait... and don't do anything until I tell you to do something," his dad instructed.

"But, Dad! Nothing is happening!" Ollie complained. He thought it was going to be quick and easy to hunt.

"Shuuuush, Ollie! You have to be patient!"

After a l-o-o-o-o-o-ng while, when Ollie had almost fallen asleep, Papa Owl suddenly whispered, "Ollie, see there....... below the berry bush? If you watch carefully, you'll see it is a mouse crawling about in the grass...."

"Yes!" Ollie relied, "I can see him!"

The very next moment Ollie jumped off the branch and quickly dived towards the mouse. But, ooooooohhhh dear, long before he came near the mouse, the little mouse saw him and disappeared under a rock.

Ollie was very upset as he flew back to his Dad high up in the tree.

"Oh, no, Dad, he got away!"

"Ollie, you did nót listen to me!" Papa Owl said in an angry voice.

"Why do you say so, Dad? You did say we were going to hunt."
"No, Ollie. I told you not to do anything until I tell you to do something. Because you've been impatient and didn't wait, the mouse managed to escape!"

"I am sorry, Dad. But I was só sure that I'd easily be able to catch him, because I can already fly very fast "

"Ollie, in real life one cannot always get hold of everything QUICKLY and IMMEDIATELY. Sometimes you have to wait if you want your reward. When you're hunting, you have to sit very still and wait very PATIENTLY... until the mouse is far away from a shelter and until he is as close to you as possible. Only then, can you charge down at your prey, as quick as lighting! The part where you catch him, only takes a few seconds, but the time of waiting can take a long, long time."
"But what if I don't have time to wait?" Ollie wanted to know.

"Then, my son, you'll go to bed hungry. If you can't learn to wait, you'll never be able to catch a mouse."

And so Ollie accompanied his dad every day. He learnt to WAIT and WAIT. Sometimes it was very difficult, but he knew he would only get it right if he listened to his dad's advice and practice hard...

As time went by, Ollie became better and better at waiting and watching... and not long after that he caught his first mouse!

"Well done, my son!" Papa Owl said to Ollie, "You have caught the mouse because you have learnt how to wait!"

Ollie learns a lesson...
(A story about Learning from your Mistakes)

One day Papa Owl said to Ollie:

"Ollie, winter is nearing and very soon it is going to be very, very cold. Your mother and I have decided that you should go and visit your grandfather for the winter season," Papa Owl explained.
"Really, Dad? I have never met Grandpa Owl," Ollie said.

Ollie had heard many stories about Grandpa Owl. Everybody in the valley knew him or at least knew of him.

Ollie greeted Mama Owl and flew side by side with Papa Owl.

"Where does Grandpa Owl live, Dad?" Ollie wanted to know.

"He lives far from here, Ollie. We'll have to fly for three full days to get there. But he lives in a country where it is a lot warmer in winter than where we live," Papa Owl explained.

"Oh-h-h, I see! In other words, you want to send me to him because it is warmer there?"

Yes, Ollie, but also because the time has come for you to learn more about life. All the young owls from this valley go to Grandpa Owl to learn from him. He is the wisest animal around and will be able to teach you many things."

After three days Ollie and his dad reached Grandpa Owl's home. He lived on top of a mountain, inside the hollowed-out bark of a giant pine tree.

"How do you do, Grandpa Owl," Ollie started. "My name is Ollie Owl and I have come to learn…"

"Ha-ha-ha!" Grandpa Owl's laughter burst out from deep in his stomach. He had a deep, deep voice.

"Seems to me this little owlet is a curious little chap. Welcome to my home, Ollie. I can see the two of us are going to get along very well!" remarked Grandpa Owl.

During the next few weeks Grandpa Owl taught Ollie many things. He taught Ollie about animals, about plants, about people and numerous other things. Grandpa also told Ollie many stories and Ollie listened carefully to every word he spoke.

One day Grandpa asked Ollie, "Ollie, have you ever made a big, big mistake?"

"No, Grandpa, I don't think so. I do not believe an owl should make mistakes."

"Is that so? And why do you say that?" Grandpa wanted to know as he pulled up his eyebrows sharply.

"Because, if an owl makes a mistake it shows he is stupid – and everyone knows that owls are very, very clever animals!" Ollie said.

"That's where you are wrong, Ollie. How do you imagine one becomes clever? One has to learn. And the only way in which an owl can really learn, is to make mistakes."

I'm afraid I don't understand, Grandpa," Ollie said. "How can an owl become cleverer if he makes mistakes? I thought that only stupid animals made mistakes."

"No, Ollie everybody makes mistakes. But the animals that learn from those mistakes – THEY become the clever ones. Let me give you an example. The very first time you went with your dad to go hunting, what happened?" Grandpa Owl asked with a smile.

"Oh dear, Grandpa, it was a disaster! I started flying much too soon and scared the mouse away! L-O-O-O-N-G before I even reached him!"

"Yes, and you didn't catch anything for a number of times, hey, Ollie?"

"That's right, Grandpa. But... how did you know that?" Ollie wanted to know, very surprised.

"Because that's what happens to every owl that learns to hunt. But because you kept on and on trying every time you made a mistake, you started getting better and better – until you caught your first mouse."

"True, Grandpa, you're right. I kept on practising. So, what you mean is that it is actually a GOOD THING to make mistakes – because I can then learn from my mistakes?" young Ollie asked.

"That's correct, Ollie. That's why you should NEVER be afraid to make mistakes. Only try not to make the same mistake twice. LEARN from your mistakes and to do better next time!"

That evening Ollie realised that he did not have to be afraid of making mistakes ever again, because that gives him the chance to learn something new..

Ollie helps a friend
(A story about helping others)

On a bright, sunny day towards the end of the winter, Ollie was flying high over the mountains. Usually Owls rest during the day and then hunt during the night, but today Ollie just felt like flying around a little. He had promised Grandpa Owl not to go too far away, and to be back home by lunch.

Ollie enjoyed flying. During the winter months he had grown a lot and now he was a young owl with strong wings. His eyes had also become sharper and sharper and he was able to see very far, even when he was very high up in the sky. He was very grateful that he had come to Grandpa Owl for the winter. Grandpa Owl had taught Ollie so many things. And besides, he was mad about Grandpa's wonderful stories.

While still flying so high, Ollie suddenly noticed a very strange thing down there, on earth.

"Is that possible?" Ollie asked himself.

He flew slightly lower and then he could clearly see that had been right. There, on the ground next to a little stream, a tiny baby bird was lying, sobbing his heart out. Quickly Ollie flew down to the ground and landed next to the little baby dove.

"Good day, Little Dove," said Ollie.

"He-he-helloo, eehh!" The little dove sobbed.

"Why are you crying so heart-brokenly?" Ollie wanted to know.

"Be-be-because my m-m-mommy was busy t t-t-teaching the seven of us young ones how to fly and then I became tired, and- and- then I sat down here, and wh-wh-when I looked again, they were all GONE! Hhhhnngggg! I thhh-think they have ffff-forgotten about me! Perhaps they didn't even notice I am not with them. Now I'll NEVER see them again. Hoo-oo-oo!"

"Have you rested enough to fly again?" Ollie asked.

"I have tried, but I am still too tired." Sighed the little dove.

"Don't you worry, little one," Ollie comforted. I will go and look for your mom and bring her to you. But first we have to hide you in a safer place. There are many foxes around and even other animals that could catch and eat you…"

Ollie then took the little dove and placed him in a small opening in a rock nearby.

"You should be safe here. Just you wait here until I come back to you." Ollie instructed.

Suddenly Ollie flew high into the blue sky. "I wonder where I'll find them?" he wondered. He flew high and low. He flew to the right and then to the left. He flew upwards and downwards. Over tree tops and through valleys he flew. Ollie was becoming tired himself.

Just as he wanted to lose courage, he saw a mommy dove with six small ones in a pine tree. Actually he heard them before he saw them for they were making such a racket that the noise could be heard from far away.

As he flew nearer he could hear them crying and shouting.

"Pardon me, doves, but why are you making this deafening noise?" he asked.

"Our little brother got lost!" the small doves shouted.

"My little boy is gone!" the mommy dove called. "We were so busy that we didn't notice that we lost him somewhere along the way..." she cried.

"There, there, it's all right," Ollie said. "I have good news for all of you. I found him and he is all right. He was just very tired and wanted to rest a little beside the stream. Come along, fly with me and I'll take you to him." Ollie said.

As soon as Ollie had brought the family together again, he flew home as quickly as possible to be in time for lunch at Grandpa's home. While eating he told Grandpa what had happened and how glad Mommy dove was when Ollie helped them.

"I'm very proud of you, Ollie! It is very important to help other animals.

We need one another and should love and care for one another. If all of us cared more and helped one another more, this world will become a much better place!"

The End